Will Shortz Presents

I CAN KENKEN!

Volume 3

KenKen™: Logic Puzzles That Make You Smarter!

Will Shortz Presents KenKen Easiest, Volume 1
Will Shortz Presents KenKen Easy, Volume 2
Will Shortz Presents KenKen Easy to Hard, Volume 3
Will Shortz Presents The Little Gift Book of KenKen

KenKen for Kids

Will Shortz Presents I Can KenKen! Volume 1
Will Shortz Presents I Can KenKen! Volume 2
Will Shortz Presents I Can KenKen! Volume 3

Will Shortz Presents

I Can KENKEN!™

VOLUME 3

75 PUZZLES FOR HAVING FUN WITH MATH

TETSUYA MIYAMOTO

Introduction by
MARILYN BURNS

ST. MARTIN'S GRIFFIN
NEW YORK

WILL SHORTZ PRESENTS I CAN KENKEN! VOLUME 3. Copyright © 2008 by Gakken Co., Ltd. All rights reserved. Printed in the United States of America. For information, address St. Martin's Press, 175 Fifth Avenue, New York, N.Y. 10010.

www.stmartins.com

ISBN-13: 978-0-312-54643-4
ISBN-10: 0-312-54643-2

First Edition: December 2008

10 9 8 7 6 5 4 3 2 1

Foreword

Lots of things in life that are good for you aren't much fun. For example, taking a bath, doing homework, getting a flu shot, going to the dentist, or eating [name any nutritious food you hate].

Conversely, lots of things in life that are fun aren't good for you, like . . . well, you can make your own list!

Then there are a few things you absolutely love—no one has to tell you to do them—that improve your health, your mind, your schoolwork, or your future.

One such thing is KenKen, a new puzzle from Japan that involves logic and numbers. I fell in love with it when I first saw it a year ago. Now, here is a whole book of KenKen puzzles to do!

The rules are simple. (Keep reading.) You can start solving in thirty seconds. KenKen takes a long time to master. But if you're like me, you won't want to put it down. At the same time as you're enjoying yourself, KenKen will sharpen you mind and improve your arithmetic skills.

If only every good thing in the world were this much fun!

—Will Shortz

Introduction

If you like solving puzzles, then this book is definitely for you.

But . . . if you think that solving puzzles isn't your kind of thing to do, don't give up on this book too quickly. KenKen puzzles may help you change your mind. Read on.

Why Solve KenKen Puzzles?

Here are reasons from kids who have learned how to KenKen. See if any of these tempt you to give KenKen puzzles a try.

"They're super fun."

"It feels really, really good when you finish one."

"I like KenKen puzzles because they wake up your brain."

"You can tell by yourself if you get the puzzle right."

"There are different ways to figure them out."

"It's fun to look for clues."

"I think KenKen is really cool."

Maybe you can add your own reason after you try KenKen puzzles for yourself. In the meantime, here's some help to get you started.

What Are KenKen Puzzles?

KenKen puzzles are puzzles you solve by writing a number in each box on a grid. The numbers you are allowed to write depend on the size of the grid. If the puzzle is a 3-by-3 grid with three boxes across and three boxes down, you can only write the numbers 1, 2, and 3. If the puzzle is a 4-by-4 grid, you can only write the numbers 1, 2, 3, and 4. For a 5-by-5 puzzle, you can only write the numbers 1, 2, 3, 4, and 5. And for a 6-by-6 puzzle, you can write the numbers 1, 2, 3, 4, 5, 6. That's the easy part.

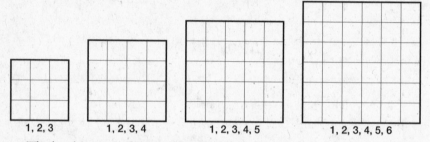

1, 2, 3   1, 2, 3, 4   1, 2, 3, 4, 5   1, 2, 3, 4, 5, 6

The harder part is figuring out where to write the numbers. There is one **Basic Rule** you must follow to solve the puzzle:

> When you write numbers in a KenKen puzzle, each row going across has to have exactly one of the numbers you can write. No repeats are allowed. And the same is true for the columns—each column going down has to have exactly one of the numbers you can write with no repeats.

> The good news is that you don't have to worry about the numbers on the diagonals, just about the numbers in the rows and columns.

OK

1	2	3
3	1	2
2	3	1

Not OK

1	2	3
2	1	3
3	2	1

But there's another challenge to solving KenKen puzzles. Not only do you have to follow the **Basic Rule**, you also have to follow the special **Number Clues**. All of the puzzles in this book are Addition KenKen puzzles or Addition/Subtraction KenKen puzzles. Let's look at this puzzle. It's a 4-by-4 Addition KenKen puzzle.

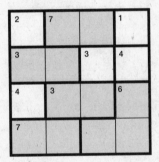

See the different shapes on the puzzle grid outlined with dark lines? And see that each outlined shape has a number written in the upper left corner? These are the special **Number Clues**.

First, about the **Number Clues** that are in outlined one-box shapes: These are lucky clues! Each of these boxes is a freebie. The **Number Clue** gives you the number to write in that box. That's it. Even though this is an Addition KenKen, no adding is needed. (That's why these are freebies!) Find the five freebies in this puzzle.

Now about the other **Number Clues**: When a number is in an outlined shape with more than one box, the number is a sum, or total. (Remember, this is an Addition KenKen puzzle.) Here's what these **Number Clues** tell you:

1. First look at the **Number Clue** 7 in the top row of the puzzle. See how this clue is in the outlined two-box shape? This **Number Clue** tells you that the two numbers you write in this shape, one in each box, have to *add up* to 7. (Remember, **Number Clues** are sums, or totals. Don't be confused and think that you are supposed to add 7 to a number—you have to think of two numbers that *add up* to 7.)

2	7		1
3		3	4
4	3		6
7			

2. Now look at the puzzle again and find the **Number Clue** 3 in the second row on the left. This clue is in an outlined two-box shape and tells you that the two numbers you write in this shape, one in each box, have to add up to 3.

2	7		1
3		3	4
4	3		6
7			

3. And when the **Number Clue** is 6—as in the outlined three-box shape in the lower right corner—it tells you that the three numbers you write in this shape, one in each box, have to add up to 6.

2	7		1
3		3	4
4	3		6
7			

Remember:
1. Follow the **Basic Rule** and be sure to write numbers without repeats in any row or column.
2. Follow the special **Number Clues** in the outlined shapes.

How to Get Started Solving a KenKen Puzzle

Now let's solve this puzzle. Here are suggestions for getting started.

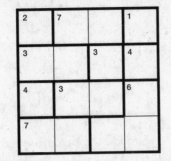

Check for freebies. This is a good first step. When you're lucky to have a freebie—one box outlined with a number in it—take advantage of the hint and write that number in the box. Be sure to check to see if a puzzle has more than one freebie. This puzzle has five freebies so you can write the numbers in each of those boxes.

Use the Number Clues. Let's start at the top with the **Number Clue** 7 in a two-box shape. Remember, since this is a 4-by-4 puzzle, the only numbers you are allowed to write in the boxes are 1, 2, 3, and 4. Only two of those numbers add up to 7—3 + 4. But . . . before you write the numbers 3 and 4 in the boxes, you have to figure out which number goes in which box. You want to be sure to follow the **Basic Rule**.

Look for other clues. Other numbers already in the puzzle, like the freebies, can give useful clues. Here the freebie 3 in the second row is a BIG help. Because this box has a 3 in it, you can't write a 3 in the box above it. That would put two 3s in the same column and break the **Basic Rule**. That's a definite no-no. So, when you write the numbers 3 and 4 in the shape in the top row with the **Number Clue** 7, you have to write the 3 in the first box and the 4 in the second box. Can you explain why this is right?

2	7		1
2	**3**	**4**	**1**
3		3	4
		3	**4**
4	3		6
4			
7			

The freebies also help you with the two missing numbers in the second row with the **Number Clue** 3. These two numbers have to add to 3, so they have to be 1 + 2. And you can't write 2 in the first box because that would put two 2s in the same column. So you have to write 1 in the first box and 2 in the second box. Can you explain why this is right?

2	7		1
2	**3**	**4**	**1**
3		3	4
1	**2**	**3**	**4**
4	3		6
4			
7			

Keep an eye out for "automatic" numbers. Sometimes you have written all but one number in a row or column. Then you can use the **Basic Rule** to see which number is missing, without having to do any other figuring. In this puzzle, the left column going down already has 2, 1, and 4 in it, so the remaining box has to be a 3. Can you explain why this is right?

2	7		1
2	**3**	**4**	**1**
3		3	4
1	**2**	**3**	**4**
4	3		6
4			
7			
3			

To finish this puzzle, you have to look for more clues. Look at the two-box shape in the lower left corner. There's already a 3 in it, and the **Number Clue** is 7, so the number in the other box has to be a 4. Or you could reason that the 4 is automatic. Can you explain why this is right?

^{2}2	^{7}3	4	^{1}1
^{3}1	2	^{3}3	^{4}4
^{4}4	^{3}		^{6}
^{7}3	4		

The three-box shape in the lower right corner has the **Number Clue** 6. That means the three numbers have to add to 6. There are a few possibilities:

1 + 2 + 3
1 + 1 + 4
2 + 2 + 2

But 2 + 2 + 2 doesn't work because it breaks the **Basic Rule** and has more than one 2 in a row or column. And the same is true for 1 + 1 + 4 since a 1 can't go in the right column going down because it has a 1 at the top, and that only leaves one box for two 1s. So 1 + 2 + 3 is it, and there is only one box possible for the 1 and one box possible for the 3. That puts 2 in the lower right corner. Can you explain why this is right?

^{2}2	^{7}3	4	^{1}1
^{3}1	2	^{3}3	^{4}4
^{4}4	^{3}		^{6}3
^{7}3	4	1	2

And you can use the "automatic" strategy to fill in the other missing numbers.

2 **2**	7 **3**	**4**	1 **1**
3 **1**	**2**	3 **3**	4 **4**
4 **4**	3 **1**	**2**	6 **3**
7 **3**	**4**	**1**	**2**

Addition/Subtraction KenKen Puzzles

The example above was an Addition KenKen puzzle. But there also are Addition/Subtraction KenKen puzzles in this book. You still have to follow the **Basic Rule** and use the **Number Clues**. But, for these puzzles, while some of the **Number Clues** are freebies and some have a plus sign, others have a minus sign. Here's an example:

1	1-		2
7+		3+	
3	1-		7+
3+		4	

As with all puzzles, first look for freebies. There are four freebies in this puzzle.

1 **1**	1-		2 **2**
7+		3+	
3 **3**	1-		7+
3+		4 **4**	

Now look at the **Number Clue** 1– in the top row. See how this clue is in the outlined two-box shape? This **Number Clue** with a minus sign tells you to think: What two numbers can I subtract to get 1? (The **Number Clue** is the answer you get when you subtract, the difference between the two numbers. Don't be confused and think that you are supposed to subtract 1 from a number—you have to think of two numbers to subtract that give the answer of 1.)

1 **1**	1-		2 **2**
7+		3+	
3 **3**	1-		7+
3+		4 **4**	

Remember that for a 4-by-4 KenKen puzzle, you can only use the numbers 1, 2, 3, and 4. There are three different ways to subtract two of these numbers to get an answer of 1:

4 – 3
3 – 2
2 – 1

Here's where the freebies help. The top row already has a 1 and a 2 in it, so the only two numbers left to write are 4 and 3. In a KenKen puzzle, either number can go first. But in this puzzle, the 4 has to go first because there already is a "freebie" 4 in the bottom row and you can't write another 4 in that same column. Can you explain why this is right?

1 **1**	1- **4**	**3**	2 **2**
7+		3+	
3 **3**	1-		7+
3+		4 **4**	

Now solve the puzzle by figuring out the rest of the numbers in the puzzle. Try the second row, with the Number Clues 7+ and 3+. Then you'll have some "automatic" numbers to write.

Some Helpful Tips

Here are some things to think about when you're solving KenKen puzzles.

- Don't rush! Solving a KenKen puzzle is not a race. The idea is to be right, not fast. Take your time, and check as you go.
- When you write an "automatic" number, be sure to check that you've also followed the clues and the numbers you wrote add up to the **Number Clue** in the shape. In the puzzle we just solved, this means being sure that the two numbers in the third row with the **Number Clue** 3—1 + 2—add up to 3. (They do!)
- Use pencil. We all make mistakes, and being able to erase is really handy. (Don't worry about making mistakes—mistakes can always help you learn more about a puzzle.) After you've solved a KenKen puzzle, then you can trace over the numbers with a pen, marker, or crayon.
- Sometimes it helps to figure out all the possible combinations of numbers that might work for the boxes in a shape, the way we did for the **Number Clue** 6 in the corner shape.

When You've Solved a Puzzle

Whenever you write numbers in all of the boxes in a KenKen puzzle, be sure to do a check. First be sure that you've followed the **Basic Rule** and there are no repeat numbers in any row or column.

Then be sure that your numbers follow the **Number Clues** and your math is correct.

For a final check, you can add the numbers in each row and column. You should get the same sum each time. For a 3-by-3 KenKen puzzle, the numbers in each row and column add up to 6; for a 4-by-4 puzzle, they add up to 10; for a 5-by-5 puzzle, they add up to 15; for a 6-by-6 puzzle, they add up to 21.

And to be absolutely sure, you can check the puzzle answer at the back of the book.

The KenKen Code

For many, many years, mathematicians have written Q.E.D. at the end of the solution to a problem. This was a signal to show that they worked on the problem, got it done, and checked to be sure the solution was right. Why Q.E.D.? The letters stand for the words in a sentence written in

Latin—Quod Erat Demonstratum. In English, this means that you have proved something to be true.

When you solve a KenKen puzzle and have checked that you are right, you can write our special KenKen signal—I.C.K.K. Or just say the letters—I, C, K, K. This is KenKen code for Q.E.D. In English, it means "I can Ken Ken!"

<table>
<tr><td>1
1</td><td>1-
4</td><td>3</td><td>2
2</td></tr>
<tr><td>7+
4</td><td>3</td><td>3+
2</td><td>1</td></tr>
<tr><td>3
3</td><td>1-
2</td><td>1</td><td>7+
4</td></tr>
<tr><td>3+
2</td><td>1</td><td>4
4</td><td>3</td></tr>
</table>

I.C.K.K.

Check the Stars on the KenKen Puzzles

You'll see that each KenKen puzzle in this book is marked with 1 star, 2 stars, or 3 stars. That's to tell you whether the puzzle is **Easy** (1 star), **Medium** (2 stars), or **Hard** (3 stars). All of the 3-by-3 KenKen puzzles are 1-star puzzles. But the size of the puzzle isn't what matters. For example, easier puzzles usually have more freebies. And harder puzzles usually have more possibilities for the numbers that can work in the boxes. So some 4-by-4 KenKen puzzles are easy, some are medium, and some are hard. And the same is true for 5-by-5 KenKen puzzles and 6-by-6 KenKen puzzles.

Pick puzzles to solve in any way you'd like. You may want to try all of the 1-star puzzles first. Or you may want to solve the puzzles by size. Or solve the KenKen puzzles in any order you'd like.

Now you're ready to KenKen! Have fun!

P.S. If you'd like to try KenKen puzzles where you just have to add, or KenKen puzzles where you have to multiply, check out volumes 1 and 2 of the I Can KenKen! books.

Difficulty Level

 Easy

⭐⭐ Medium

⭐⭐⭐ Hard

+ **1**

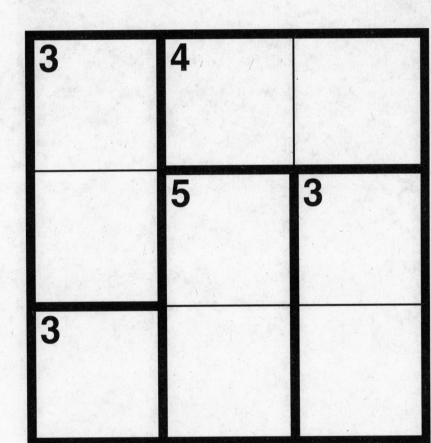

3	**4**	
	5	**3**
3		

Remember, fill in "freebies" first!

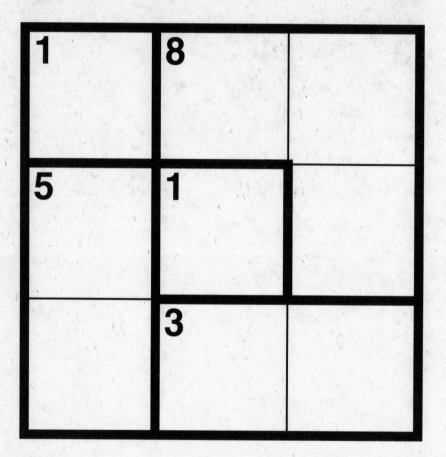

1	8	
5	1	
	3	

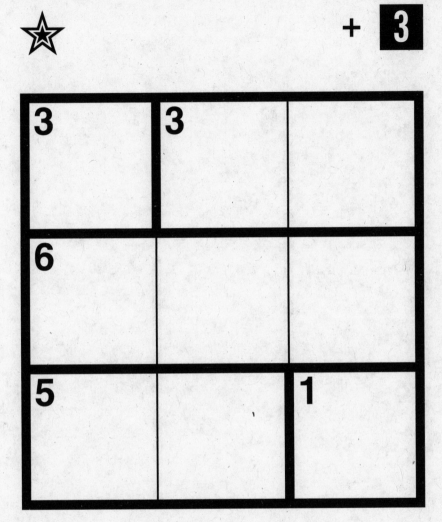

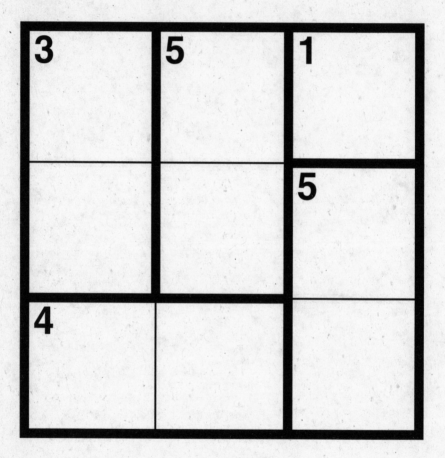

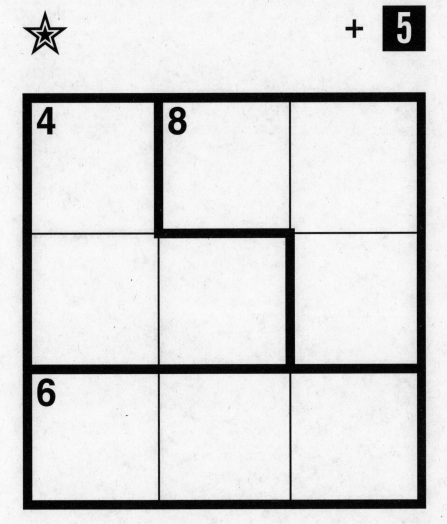

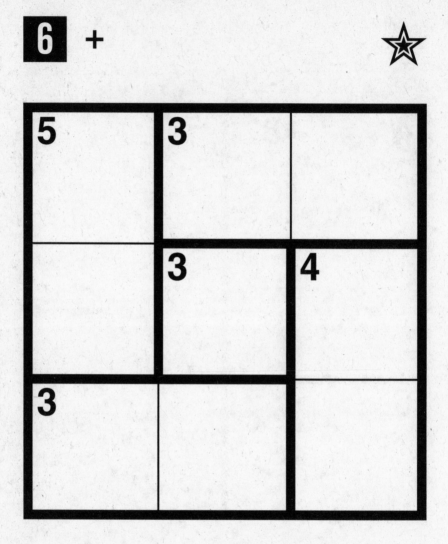

+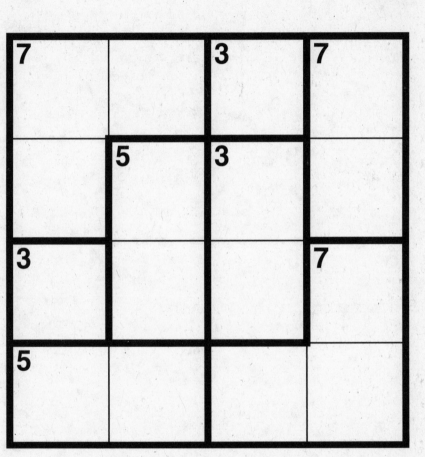

7		3	7
	5	3	
3			7
5			

Level up! Now you use numbers 1, 2, 3, and 4!

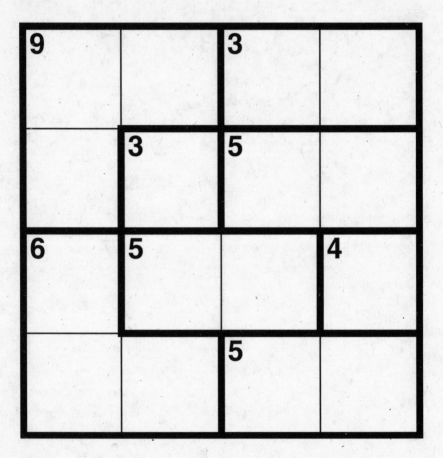

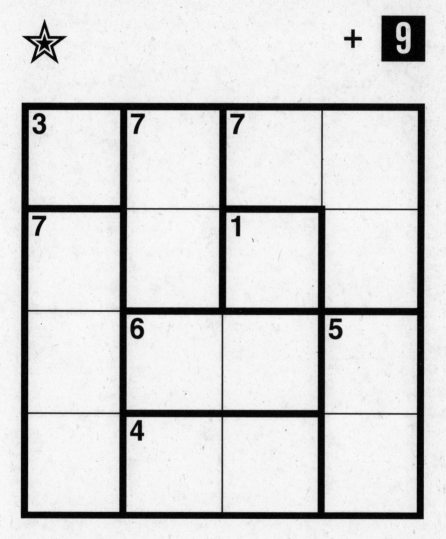

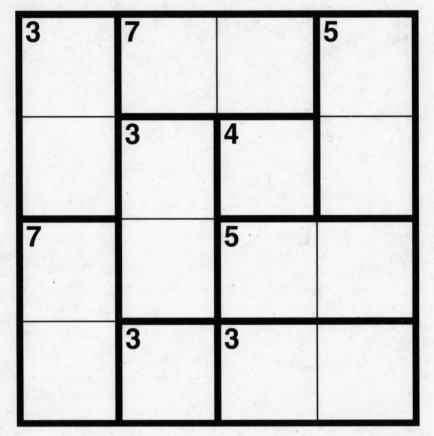

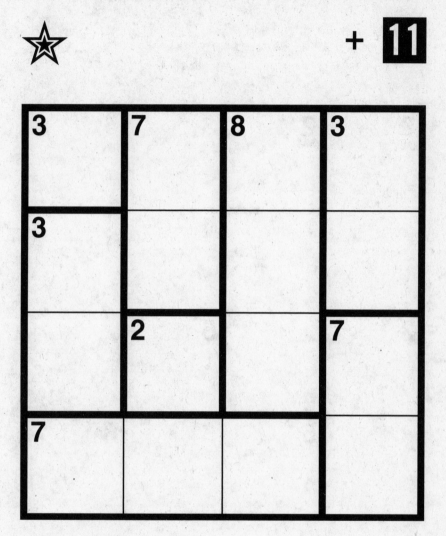

12 +

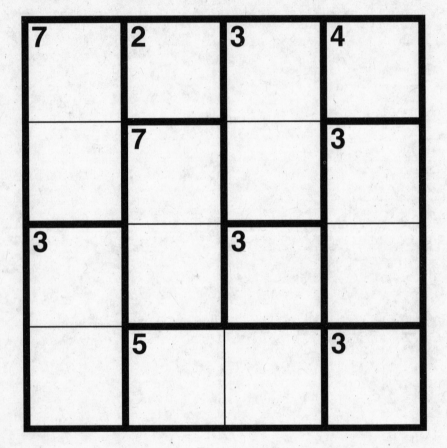

7	2	3	4
	7		3
3		3	
	5		3

+ **13**

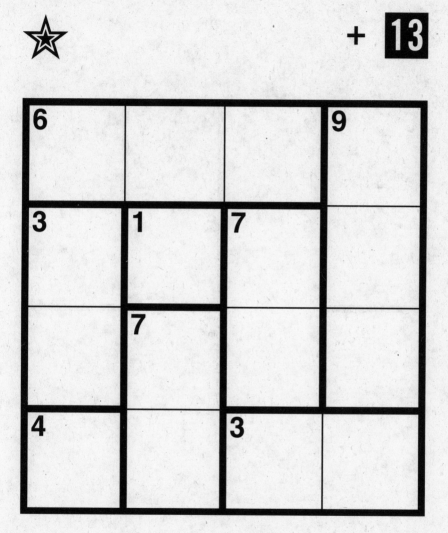

14 +

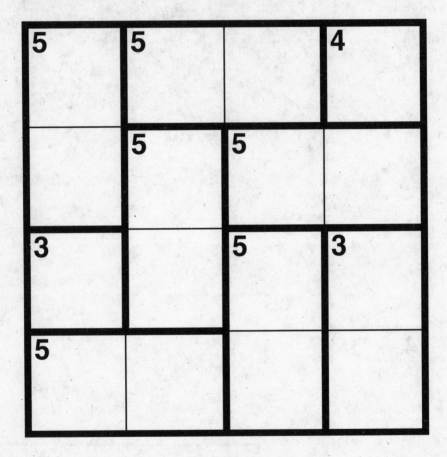

3	3		7
3	1	7	
	7		2
4		3	

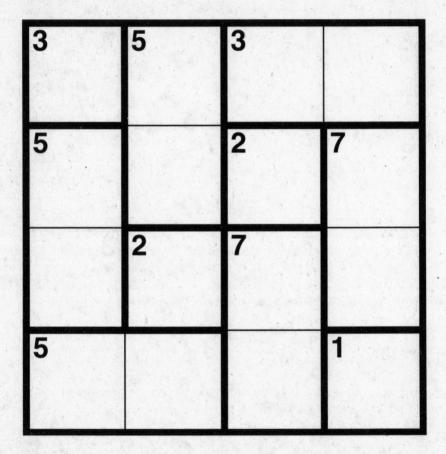

+ **17**

5	5		4
	3	4	
5		4	3
	7		

5		3	3
4	5	3	
5			4
	1	7	

1	7		3
7	3	3	
	3		7
2		4	

20 +

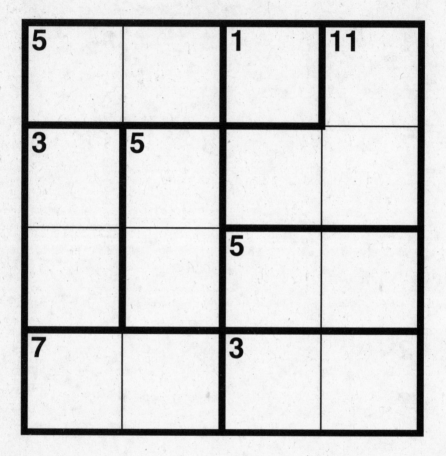

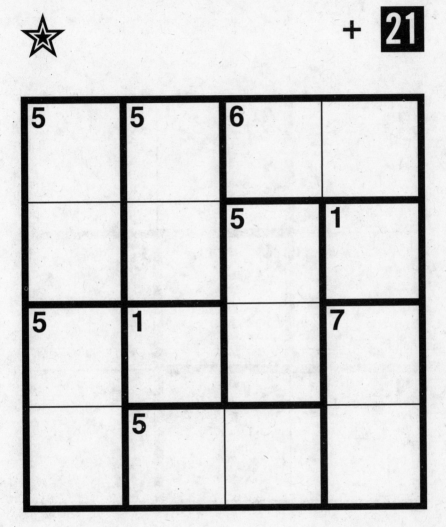

22 +/−

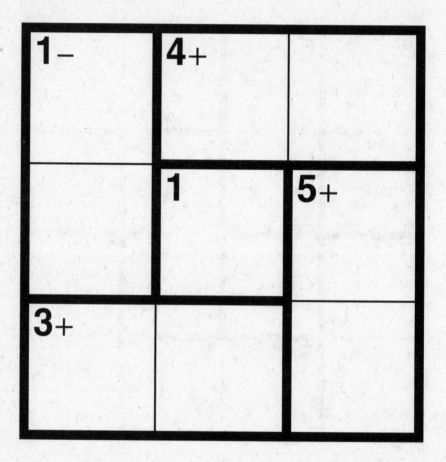

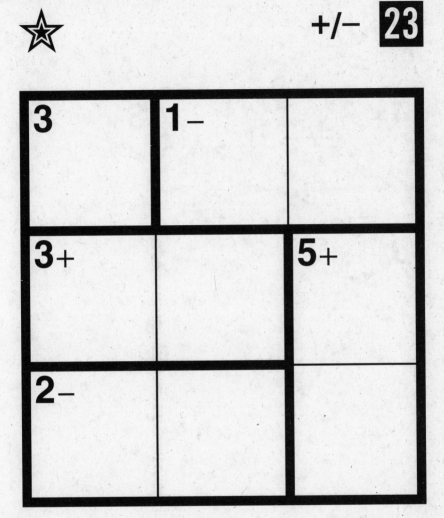

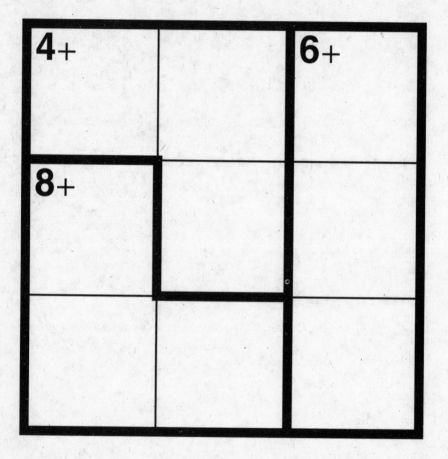

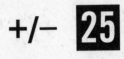
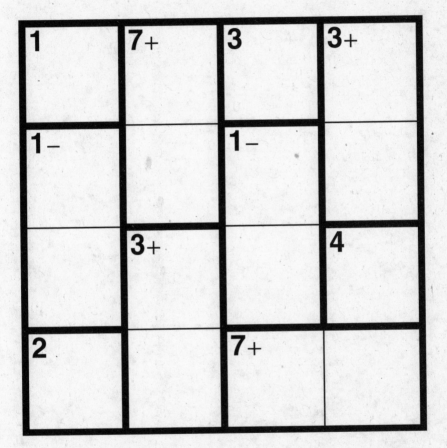

1	**7+**	**3**	**3+**
1−		**1−**	
	3+		**4**
2		**7+**	

Level up! Now you use numbers 1, 2, 3, and 4!

26 +/−

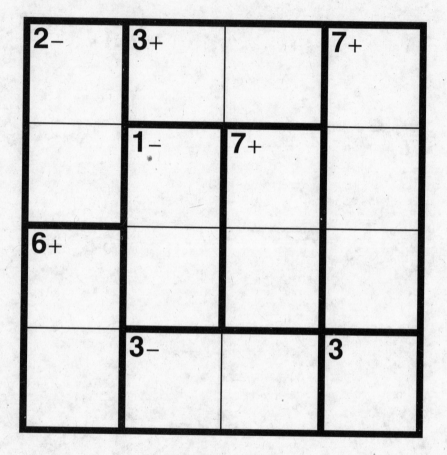

+/− **27**

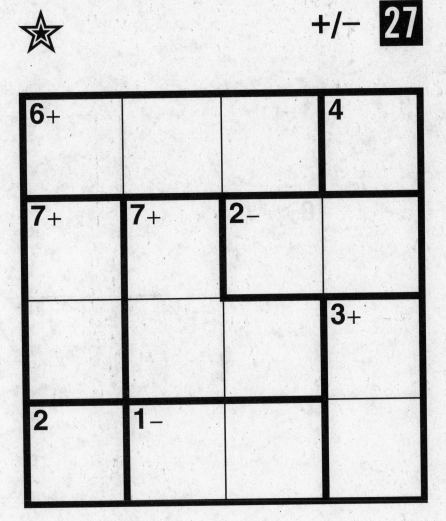

28 +/−

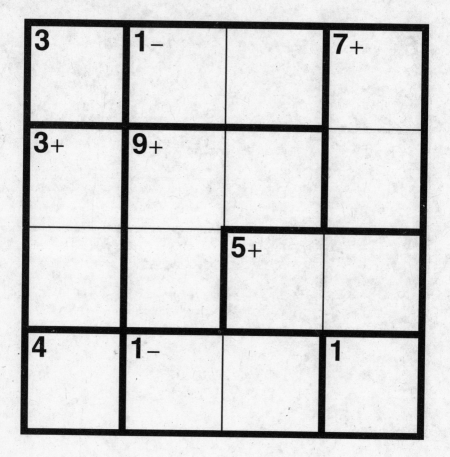

+/− **29**

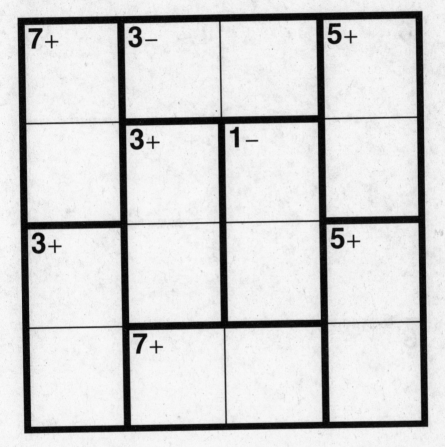

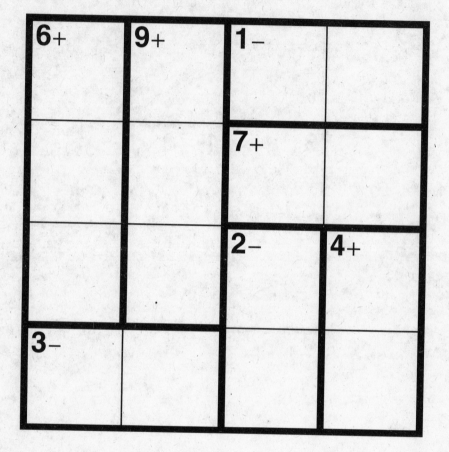

6+	9+	1−	
		7+	
		2−	4+
3−			

+/− **31**

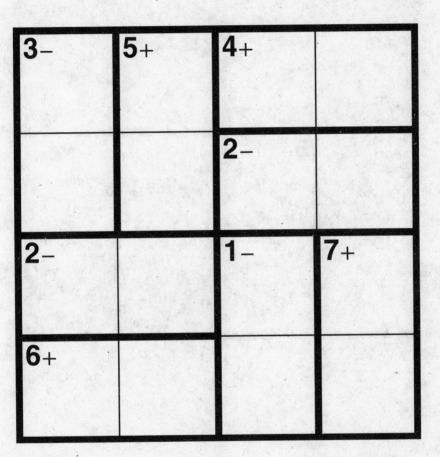

32 +/−

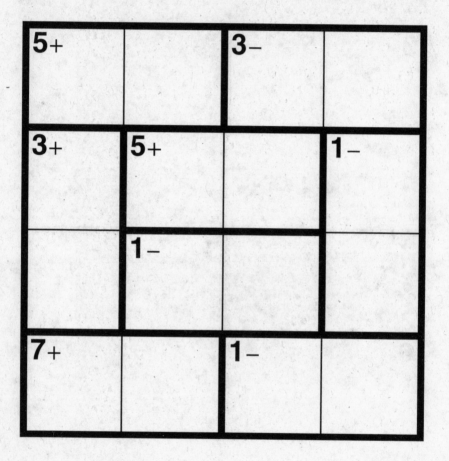

 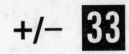

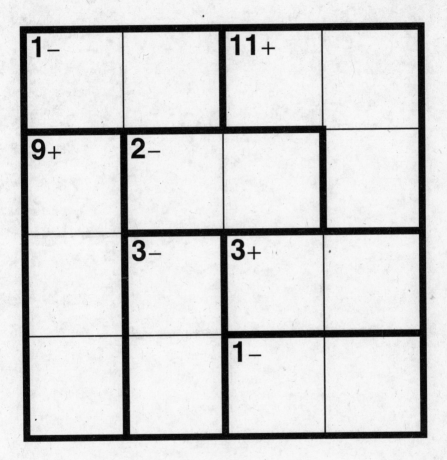

34 +/−

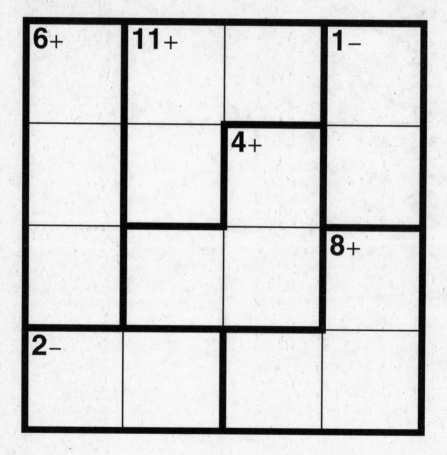

6+ | 11+ | | 1−

4+

8+

2−

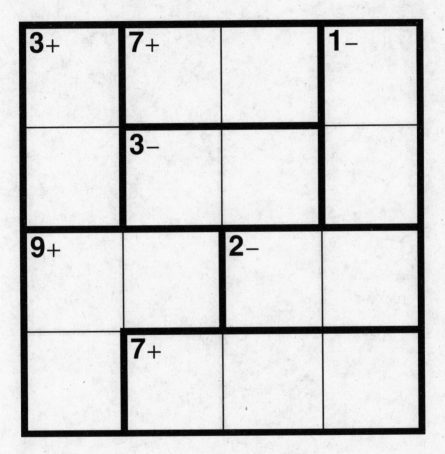

36 +/−

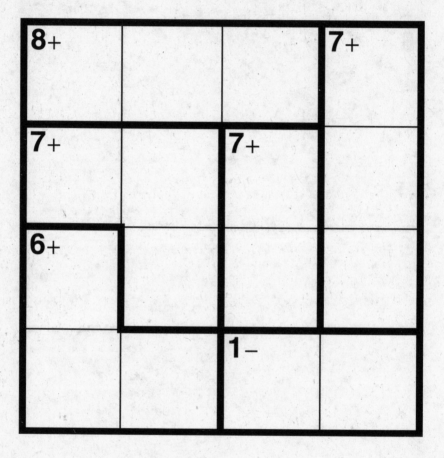

1−	8+		
	9+		1−
12+			
		3−	

38 +/−

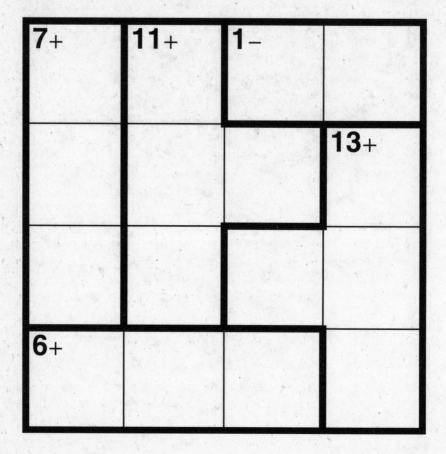

3−		**12**+	
9+	**7**+		
			1−
	2−		

40 +/− ★★★

1−	2−		7+
	9+		
8+			
		5+	

+/− **41**

1−		**6**+	
3−			**8**+
	7+	**1**−	

9+	4	3+		1−
	8+		1	
2	4−	1−		9+
2−		6+	3	
	2		4−	

Level up! Now you use numbers 1, 2, 3, 4, and 5!

9+		1−	4−	3
3−	3			2−
	8+		2	
1−	2	9+		1
	3−		8+	

44 +/−

4−	3+	6+		3
		7+	9+	
2−	3		2−	5
	9+	1		1−
3		7+		

8+		3+	4	4−
4	3+		5+	
4+		5		4
	7+		3−	
2	9+		2−	

1−		8+		4
5	7+		1	1−
4+	9+		2−	
	1−	1		4−
4		3−		

+/− **47**

6+		7+	2	5+
5	1−		6+	
7+		2		6+
	2	4−	4	
1−			1−	

48 +/− ★ ★

2	**8+**	**3−**		**5**
7+		**1**	**5+**	
	6+	**7+**		**3−**
4−		**3**	**9+**	
	3+			**3**

+/− **49**

1−		7+		5
4	8+	4+	7+	
2−			2	3−
	2	9+		
9+		1−		3

50 +/−

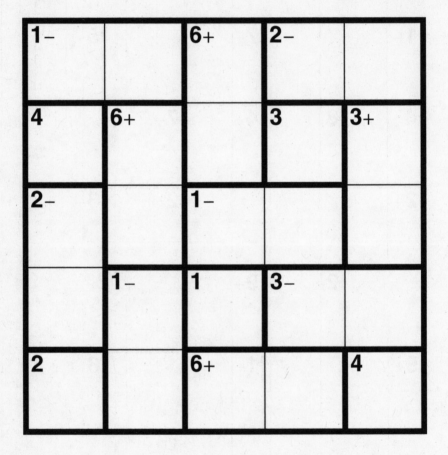

1−		6+	2−	
4	6+		3	3+
2−		1−		
	1−	1	3−	
2		6+		4

+/− **51**

1	8+		5+	9+
6+		3+		
8+			3−	
9+	2	5+		5+
	2−		5	

52 +/−

7+	**4**−	**3**−		**3**
		4	**3**+	
3−	**6**+	**8**+		**3**−
		1−	**3**	
2−			**9**+	

+/− **53**

4−		8+	2	3−
5+	3		9+	
	5+			3−
3+		1−		
4	3−		4+	

54 +/−

1−		9+		1
2	4−	7+		1−
6+		3	1−	
	4	3+		5+
7+			5	

★★★ +/− 55

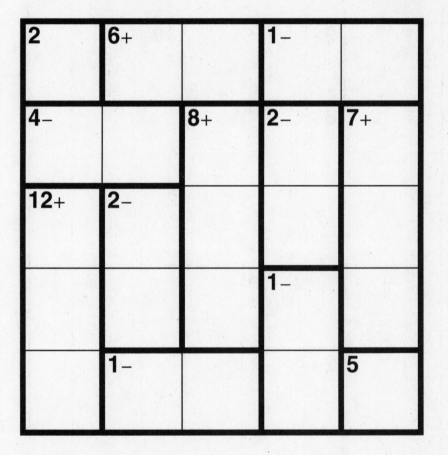

2	6+		1−	
4−		8+	2−	7+
12+	2−			
			1−	
	1−			5

56 +/−

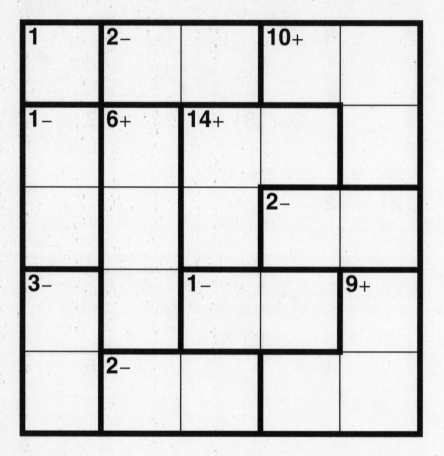

1	2−		10+	
1−	6+	14+		
			2−	
3−		1−		9+
	2−			

+/− **57**

1−		12+	3−	
1−	4−		8+	
			7+	
9+		6+		
1−			3−	

58 +/−

4−		9+	2	1−
6+			12+	
	10+			6+
	12+			
		1−		

9+		8+		10+
1−	6+			
			12+	
1−	4−			
	9+		1−	

60 +/−

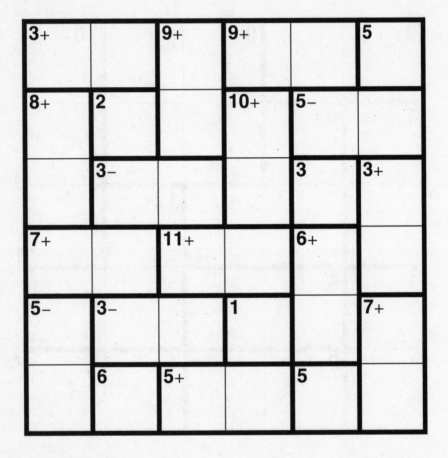

3+		9+	9+		5
8+	2		10+	5−	
	3−			3	3+
7+		11+		6+	
5−	3−		1		7+
	6	5+		5	

Level up! Now you use numbers 1, 2, 3, 4, 5, and 6!

+/− **61**

9+		5+		6	5−
3	10+	1	3−		
11+		1−	9+	3+	
	1			2−	3
1−		5−			9+
3+		11+		3	

62 +/−

10+		2	4+		5
3−	10+		4−		3−
	1	7+		5+	
4−		4	11+		3+
1	2−			4	
8+		3+		10+	

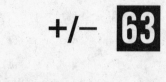
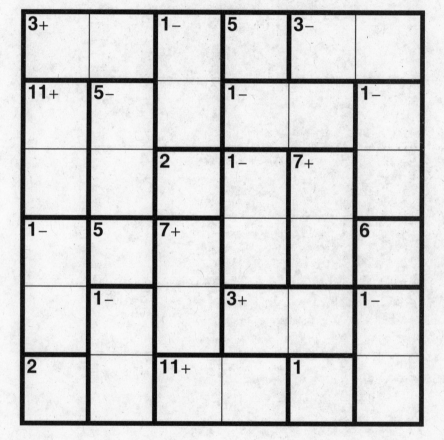

64 +/−

4−		11+	3	3−	
2−			2−		4−
9+	3	4−		4	
	1−		2−		6
2−		3	3+	3−	
1	9+			3−	

+/− **65**

11+		7+	1	7+	
3	2−		5+		4−
9+		5−		5+	
	3	10+	2−		1
3+				11+	
5−		3	3−		4

66 +/−

1	1−	7+	1−	9+	
1−				5	1−
	4−		1−		
1−	4−		2	1−	6
	4	7+			9+
1−		5	7+		

+/− **67**

1	5+	7+	1−		2
1−			4	1−	7+
	1−		5+		
2−		7+		5+	5
5+	5		7+		7+
	9+			1	

68 +/−

13+			3−		14+
3+		9+	3−		
5+			4	3+	
4	13+	11+			1
4−		5−		1−	
		5+		9+	

+/− 69

4	11+	3+		5−	7+
4−		8+	6+		
	9+			9+	
5+		15+			3+
		3−	11+		
5−			5+		5

+/−

3−		2	11+		8+
9+	10+		3+		
	3	10+			2
9+	3+	14+	7+		5−
			4+	2	
3−				10+	

+/− **71**

6+	11+		1−	9+	3+
	10+	4−			
			3−	3−	
9+	3+			5−	12+
	11+				
3−		7+			

72 +/−

3+	11+		1−		1
7+	7+			1−	11+
11+		3−			
	9+	3−		3−	
1−		3+	11+		5+
			9+		

13+		10+		4−	
	3+		8+		15+
3−		3−			
	16+		5−		8+
		6+			
11+			9+		

74 +/−

3+		10+		10+	
7+	11+			6+	
	3−	4−			3−
17+		7+	1−		
			7+		3−
5+			5−		

11+		4+		7+	7+
1−	13+				
	7+	4−			9+
5−		1−	9+		
			11+		8+
9+		8+			

CONGRATULATIONS!

_____

(print name here)

You have just completed
**I Can KenKen! Volume 3!**
In doing so, you mastered seventy-five
killer KenKen puzzles from small 3 x 3 grids to
giant 6 x 6 grids using addition and subtraction.

YOU'VE OFFICIALLY ACHIEVED THE RANK OF
KENKEN CRUSADER

ANSWERS

1

³2	⁴1	3
1	⁵3	³2
³3	2	1

2

¹1	⁸3	2
⁵2	¹1	3
3	³2	1

3

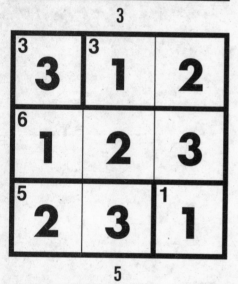

³3	³1	2
⁶1	2	3
⁵2	3	¹1

4

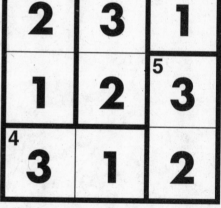

³2	⁵3	¹1
1	2	⁵3
⁴3	1	2

5

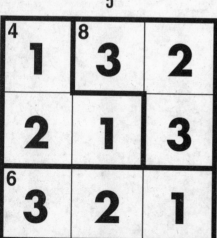

⁴1	⁸3	2
2	1	3
⁶3	2	1

6

⁵3	³1	2
2	³3	⁴1
³1	2	3

[7] 1	2	[3] 3	[7] 4
4	[5] 1	[3] 2	3
[3] 3	4	1	[7] 2
[5] 2	3	4	1

[9] 3	4	[3] 1	2
2	[3] 3	[5] 4	1
[6] 1	[5] 2	3	[4] 4
4	1	[5] 2	3

[3] 3	[7] 4	[7] 2	1
[7] 2	3	[1] 1	4
1	[6] 2	4	[5] 3
4	[4] 1	3	2

[3] 1	[7] 4	3	[5] 2
2	[3] 1	[4] 4	3
[7] 3	2	[5] 1	4
4	[3] 3	[3] 2	1

[3] 3	[7] 4	[8] 1	[3] 2
[3] 2	3	4	1
1	[2] 2	3	[7] 4
[7] 4	1	2	3

[7] 3	[2] 2	[3] 1	[4] 4
4	[7] 3	2	[3] 1
[3] 1	4	[3] 3	2
2	[5] 1	4	[3] 3

13

3	2	1	4
2	1	4	3
1	4	3	2
4	3	2	1

14

1	2	3	4
4	1	2	3
3	4	1	2
2	3	4	1

15

3	2	1	4
2	1	4	3
1	4	3	2
4	3	2	1

16

3	4	1	2
4	1	2	3
1	2	3	4
2	3	4	1

17

1	3	2	4
4	2	1	3
3	1	4	2
2	4	3	1

18

1	4	3	2
4	3	2	1
3	2	1	4
2	1	4	3

¹1	⁷4	3	³2
⁷4	³3	³2	1
3	³2	1	⁷4
²2	1	⁴4	3

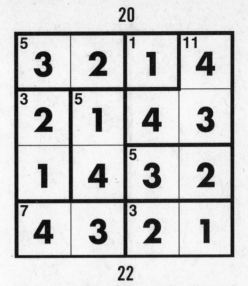

⁵3	2	¹1	¹¹4
³2	⁵1	4	3
1	4	⁵3	2
⁷4	3	³2	1

⁵1	⁵3	⁶4	2
4	2	⁵3	¹1
⁵3	¹1	2	⁷4
2	⁵4	1	3

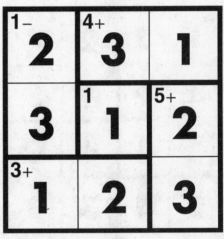

1− 2	4+ 3	1
3	1 1	5+ 2
3+ 1	2	3

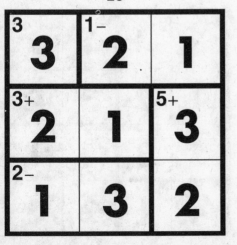

3 3	1− 2	1
3+ 2	1	5+ 3
2− 1	3	2

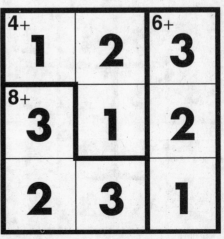

4+ 1	2	6+ 3
8+ 3	1	2
2	3	1

25

¹1	⁷⁺4	³3	³⁺2
¹⁻4	3	¹⁻2	1
3	³⁺2	1	⁴4
²2	1	⁷⁺4	3

26

²⁻3	³⁺1	2	⁷⁺4
1	¹⁻3	⁷⁺4	2
⁶⁺4	2	3	1
2	³⁻4	1	³3

27

⁶⁺1	3	2	⁴4
⁷⁺4	⁷⁺2	²⁻1	3
3	1	4	³⁺2
²2	¹⁻4	3	1

28

³3	¹⁻2	1	⁷⁺4
³⁺2	⁹⁺1	4	3
1	4	⁵⁺3	2
⁴4	¹⁻3	2	¹1

29

⁷⁺3	³⁻4	1	⁵⁺2
4	³⁺1	¹⁻2	3
³⁺1	2	3	⁵⁺4
2	⁷⁺3	4	1

30

⁶⁺3	⁹⁺4	¹⁻1	2
1	2	⁷⁺3	4
2	3	²⁻4	⁴⁺1
³⁻4	1	2	3

31

3− 4	5+ 2	4+ 3	1
1	3	2− 4	2
2− 3	1	1− 2	7+ 4
6+ 2	4	1	3

32

5+ 3	2	3− 1	4
3+ 2	5+ 1	4	1− 3
1	1− 4	3	2
7+ 4	3	1− 2	1

33

1− 1	2	11+ 4	3
9+ 2	2− 3	1	4
3	3− 4	3+ 2	1
4	1	1− 3	2

34

6+ 1	11+ 3	4	1− 2
2	4	4+ 1	3
3	1	2	8+ 4
2− 4	2	3	1

35

3+ 1	7+ 3	4	1− 2
2	3− 4	1	3
9+ 4	2	2− 3	1
3	7+ 1	2	4

36

8+ 3	4	1	7+ 2
7+ 2	3	7+ 4	1
6+ 1	2	3	4
4	1	1− 2	3

37

1− **2**	8+ **1**	**4**	**3**
1	9+ **4**	**3**	1− **2**
12+ **4**	**3**	**2**	**1**
3	**2**	3− **1**	**4**

38

7+ **4**	11+ **3**	1− **2**	**1**
1	**4**	**3**	13+ **2**
2	**1**	**4**	**3**
6+ **3**	**2**	**1**	**4**

39

3− **1**	**4**	12+ **2**	**3**
9+ **2**	7+ **1**	**3**	**4**
3	**2**	**4**	1− **1**
4	2− **3**	**1**	**2**

40

1− **4**	2− **3**	**1**	7+ **2**
3	9+ **2**	**4**	**1**
8+ **2**	**1**	**3**	**4**
1	**4**	5+ **2**	**3**

41

1− **3**	**4**	6+ **1**	**2**
3− **4**	**1**	**2**	8+ **3**
1	7+ **2**	1− **3**	**4**
2	**3**	**4**	**1**

42

9+ **5**	4 **4**	3+ **1**	**2**	1− **3**
4	8+ **3**	**5**	1 **1**	**2**
2 **2**	4− **1**	1− **3**	**4**	9+ **5**
2− **1**	**5**	6+ **2**	3 **3**	**4**
3	2 **2**	**4**	4− **5**	**1**

43

9+ 5	4	1- 2	4- 1	3 3
3- 4	3 3	1	5	2- 2
1	8+ 5	3	2 2	4
1- 3	2 2	9+ 5	4	1 1
2	3- 1	4	8+ 3	5

44

4- 5	3+ 1	6+ 2	4	3 3
1	2	7+ 3	9+ 5	4
2- 2	3 3	4	2- 1	5 5
4	9+ 5	1 1	3	1- 2
3 3	4	7+ 5	2	1

45

8+ 5	3	3+ 2	4 4	4- 1
4 4	3+ 2	1	5+ 3	5
4+ 3	1	5 5	2	4 4
1	7+ 4	3	3- 5	2
2 2	9+ 5	4	2- 1	3

46

1- 2	1	8+ 5	3	4 4
5 5	7+ 4	3	1 1	1- 2
4+ 1	9+ 5	4	2- 2	3
3	1- 2	1 1	4	4- 5
4 4	3	3- 2	5	1

47

6+ 1	5	7+ 4	2 2	5+ 3
5 5	1- 4	3	6+ 1	2
7+ 4	3	2 2	5	6+ 1
3	2 2	4- 1	4 4	5
1- 2	1	5	1- 3	4

48

2 2	8+ 3	3- 4	1	5 5
7+ 4	5	1 1	5+ 3	2
3	6+ 4	7+ 5	2	3- 1
4- 1	2	3 3	9+ 5	4
5	3+ 1	2	4	3 3

49

1- 2	1	7+ 4	3	5 5
4 4	8+ 3	4+ 1	7+ 5	2
2- 1	5	3	2 2	3- 4
3	2 2	9+ 5	4	1
9+ 5	4	1- 2	1	3 3

50

1- 1	2	6+ 4	2- 5	3
4 4	6+ 5	2	3 3	3+ 1
2- 5	1	1- 3	4	2
3	1- 4	1 1	3- 2	5
2 2	3	6+ 5	1	4 4

51

1 1	8+ 3	5	5+ 2	9+ 4
6+ 2	4	3+ 1	3	5
8+ 3	5	2	3- 4	1
9+ 5	2 2	5+ 4	1	5+ 3
4	2- 1	3	5 5	2

52

7+ 4	4- 1	3- 5	2	3 3
3	5	4 4	3+ 1	2
3- 2	6+ 4	8+ 3	5	3- 1
5	2	1- 1	3 3	4
2- 1	3	2	9+ 4	5

53

4- 5	1	8+ 3	2 2	3- 4
5+ 2	3 3	5	9+ 4	1
3	5+ 4	1	5	3- 2
3+ 1	2	1- 4	3	5
4 4	3- 5	2	4+ 1	3

54

1- 3	2	9+ 5	4	1 1
2 2	4- 1	7+ 4	3	1- 5
6+ 1	5	3 3	1- 2	4
5	4 4	3+ 2	1	5+ 3
7+ 4	3	1	5 5	2

55

2:2	6+:1	5	1-:4	3
4-:1	5	8+:4	2-:3	7+:2
12+:3	2-:2	1	5	4
5	4	3	1-:2	1
4	1-:3	2	1	5:5

56

1:1	2-:4	2	10+:3	5
1-:3	6+:1	14+:4	5	2
4	2	5	2-:1	3
3-:5	3	1-:1	2	9+:4
2	2-:5	3	4	1

57

1-:3	2	12+:5	3-:1	4
1-:2	4-:1	4	8+:5	3
1	5	3	7+:4	2
9+:5	4	6+:2	3	1
1-:4	3	1	3-:2	5

58

4-:5	1	9+:3	2:2	1-:4
6+:1	2	4	12+:3	5
3	10+:4	1	5	6+:2
2	12+:3	5	4	1
4	5	1-:2	1	3

59

9+:5	4	8+:3	2	10+:1
1-:4	6+:3	2	1	5
3	2	1	12+:5	4
1-:2	4-:1	5	4	3
1	9+:5	4	1-:3	2

60

3+:2	1	9+:4	9+:3	6	5:5
8+:3	2:2	5	10+:4	5-:1	6
5	3-:4	1	6	3:3	3+:2
7+:4	3	11+:6	5	6+:2	1
5-:6	3-:5	2	1:1	4	7+:3
1	6:6	5+:3	2	5:5	4

61

[9+]4	5	[5+]2	3	[6]6	[5-]1
[3]3	[10+]4	[1]1	[3-]2	5	6
[11+]5	6	[1-]3	[9+]4	[3+]1	2
6	[1]1	4	5	[2-]2	[3]3
[1-]2	3	[5-]6	1	4	[9+]5
[3+]1	2	[11+]5	6	[3]3	4

62

[10+]4	6	[2]2	[4+]3	1	[5]5
[3-]2	[10+]4	6	[4-]1	5	[3-]3
5	[1]1	[7+]3	4	[5+]2	6
[4-]6	2	[4]4	[11+]5	3	[3+]1
[1]1	[2-]3	5	6	[4]4	2
[8+]3	5	[3+]1	2	[10+]6	4

63

[3+]1	2	[1-]4	[5]5	[3-]6	3
[11+]6	[5-]1	3	[1-]4	5	[1-]2
5	6	[2]2	[1-]3	[7+]4	1
[1-]4	[5]5	[7+]1	2	3	[6]6
3	[1-]4	6	[3+]1	2	[1-]5
[2]2	3	[11+]5	6	[1]1	4

64

[4-]2	6	[11+]5	[3]3	[3-]1	4
[2-]3	1	6	[2-]4	2	[4-]5
[9+]5	[3]3	[4-]2	6	[4]4	1
4	[1-]2	1	[2-]5	3	[6]6
[2-]6	4	[3]3	[3+]1	[3-]5	2
[1]1	[9+]5	4	2	[3-]6	3

65

[11+]6	5	[7+]2	[1]1	[7+]4	3
[3]3	[2-]2	5	[5+]4	1	[4-]6
[9+]5	4	[5-]1	6	[5+]3	2
4	[3]3	[10+]6	[2-]5	2	[1]1
[3+]2	1	4	3	[11+]6	5
[5-]1	6	[3]3	[3-]2	5	4

66

[1]1	[1-]2	[7+]4	[1-]5	[9+]6	3
[1-]6	1	3	4	[5]5	[1-]2
5	[4-]6	2	[1-]3	4	1
[1-]4	[4-]5	1	[2]2	[1-]3	[6]6
3	[4]4	[7+]6	1	2	[9+]5
[1-]2	3	[5]5	[7+]6	1	4

67

¹1	⁵⁺3	⁷⁺4	¹⁻5	6	²2
¹⁻6	2	3	⁴4	¹⁻5	⁷⁺1
5	¹⁻1	2	⁵⁺3	4	6
²⁻4	6	⁷⁺1	2	⁵⁺3	⁵5
⁵⁺3	⁵5	6	⁷⁺1	2	⁷⁺4
2	⁹⁺4	5	6	¹1	3

68

¹³⁺6	5	2	³⁻1	4	¹⁴⁺3
³⁺2	1	⁹⁺4	³⁻3	6	5
⁵⁺3	2	5	⁴4	³⁺1	6
⁴4	¹³⁺3	¹¹⁺6	5	2	¹1
⁴⁻5	4	⁵⁻1	6	¹⁻3	2
1	6	⁵⁺3	2	⁹⁺5	4

69

⁴4	¹¹⁺5	³⁺2	1	⁵⁻6	⁷⁺3
⁴⁻5	6	⁸⁺3	⁶⁺2	1	4
1	⁹⁺2	5	4	⁹⁺3	6
⁵⁺2	3	¹⁵⁺6	5	4	³⁺1
3	4	³⁻1	¹¹⁺6	5	2
⁵⁻6	1	4	⁵⁺3	2	⁵5

70

³⁻1	4	²2	¹¹⁺6	5	⁸⁺3
⁹⁺3	¹⁰⁺6	4	³⁺2	1	5
6	³3	¹⁰⁺1	5	4	²2
⁹⁺5	³⁺2	¹⁴⁺6	⁷⁺4	3	⁵⁻1
4	1	5	⁴⁺3	²2	6
³⁻2	5	3	¹⁰⁺1	6	4

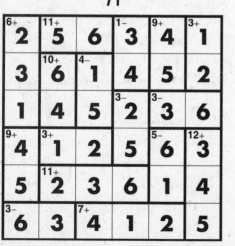

71

⁶⁺2	¹¹⁺5	6	¹⁻3	⁹⁺4	³⁺1
3	¹⁰⁺6	⁴⁻1	4	5	2
1	4	5	³⁻2	³⁻3	6
⁹⁺4	³⁺1	2	5	⁵⁻6	¹²⁺3
5	¹¹⁺2	3	6	1	4
³⁻6	3	⁷⁺4	1	2	5

72

³⁺2	¹¹⁺5	6	¹⁻3	4	¹1
1	⁷⁺4	⁷⁺5	2	¹⁻3	¹¹⁺6
¹¹⁺6	3	³⁻4	1	2	5
5	⁹⁺2	³⁻3	6	1	4
¹⁻4	1	³⁺2	¹¹⁺5	6	⁵⁺3
3	6	1	⁹⁺4	5	2

73

¹³⁺3	4	¹⁰⁺1	5	⁴⁻6	2
6	³⁺1	4	⁸⁺2	3	¹⁵⁺5
³⁻1	2	³⁻5	3	4	6
4	¹⁶⁺5	2	⁵⁻6	1	⁸⁺3
5	6	⁶⁺3	1	2	4
¹¹⁺2	3	6	⁹⁺4	5	1

74

³⁺1	2	¹⁰⁺3	5	¹⁰⁺6	4
⁷⁺4	¹¹⁺5	6	2	⁶⁺3	1
3	³⁻4	⁴⁻5	1	2	³⁻6
¹⁷⁺6	1	⁷⁺2	¹⁻4	5	3
5	6	1	⁷⁺3	4	³⁻2
⁵⁺2	3	4	⁵⁻6	1	5

75

¹¹⁺5	6	⁴⁺1	3	⁷⁺4	⁷⁺2
¹⁻2	¹³⁺3	4	6	1	5
3	⁷⁺4	⁴⁻5	1	2	⁹⁺6
⁵⁻6	1	¹⁻2	⁹⁺4	5	3
1	2	3	¹¹⁺5	6	⁸⁺4
⁹⁺4	5	⁸⁺6	2	3	1

For Parents, Teachers, and Other Adults

KenKen puzzles were created by a Japanese educator, Tetsuya Miyamoto. In Japanese they are called KenKen, which translates as "cleverness squared." When I first learned about KenKen puzzles, I was intrigued. As a teacher of elementary and middle school mathematics for more than forty years, I became excited by their potential. And when I introduced them in several different grade levels, I was delighted to see how the puzzles instantly engaged students' interest and curiosity. Working on KenKen puzzles encourages children to concentrate and persevere.

Figuring out solutions to KenKen puzzles relies on basic math facts, thus providing beneficial practice in the context of solving puzzles. What I particularly like about these puzzles is that they also encourage children to think and reason mathematically, and to do so in their own ways. While each puzzle has one correct solution, there is no one "right" way to tackle it. In fact, I've found that I can solve the same problem in more than one way, depending on the order I use when choosing clues.

In some ways, KenKen puzzles are similar to the popular sudoku puzzles. Both involve filling in a grid with numbers, and both call for solutions without repeating numbers in the same row or column. But there is an important difference that makes KenKen puzzles particularly valuable for teaching mathematics. While numbers are used in sudoku puzzles, they are merely placeholder symbols; that is, the puzzles could use the letters of the alphabet, or pictures of fruit, or any other symbols and the structure of the sudoku puzzle would still be the same. In KenKen puzzles, however, number relationships are integral to solutions. The puzzles in this book call for adding and subtracting; puzzles in other of the I Can KenKen! books call for multiplying, and later for dividing as well. When solving KenKen puzzles, children get practice with basic arithmetic facts in a problem-solving context that provides a reason for using math.

The mechanics for the puzzles aren't complicated for children to learn. If you've not tried solving KenKen puzzles yourself, read through the introduction to familiarize yourself with the KenKen puzzles in this book. (I based this introduction on my actual experience introducing the puzzles in classrooms, and I've found that the introduction is also suitable for adults just getting started.)

An Additional Hint

There's one aspect of subtraction clues that I've found initially stump some children, which is that the numbers can be written in any order. For example, look at this 4-by-4 Addition/Subtraction KenKen puzzle. It has two freebie Number Clues, and those numbers are written in. The two-box shape in the upper left corner has the Number Clue of 3−.

3−	1−		4 **4**
	7+	4+	
5+		7+	
		3 **3**	

This clue means that the answer you get when you subtract the numbers in these two boxes, the difference, has to be 3. Using just the numbers 1, 2, 3, and 4, since these are the only numbers allowed in a 4-by-4 puzzle, the only two numbers that are possible are 1 and 4 because $4 - 1 = 3$. But since there already is a 4 in the top row, because of the freebie clue, the 1 has to be written above the 4. And this bothers some children.

3- **1**	1-		4 **4**
4	7+	4+	
5+		7+	
		3 **3**	

In contrast, the Number Clue for the other two-box shape in the first column is 5+. Here there are two possible combinations—4 + 1 and 3 + 2. But since the column already has 4 and 1 in it, the only possibility is 3 + 2. The freebie in the bottom row is the clue for writing the 3 above the 2 in this shape. But even if the 2 went above the 3, children wouldn't be bothered because they've learned that they can add numbers in any order and get the same answer—3 + 2 and 2 + 3. (That's because of the Commutative Property of Addition.)

3- **1**	1-		4 **4**
4	7+	4+	
5+ **3**		7+	
2		**3**	

It may help to remind children that with the subtraction clues, the difference is what the clue tells, not the order in which the numbers appear in the puzzle.

Now try completing this KenKen puzzle.

Both in and out of the classroom, KenKen puzzles make a valuable contribution to students' learning. They help cement basic math facts, build number sense, promote logical thinking, build problem-solving skills, and motivate students mathematically in new and engaging ways.

Good luck with these KenKen puzzles!

—Marilyn Burns